M000308145

Lost On My Own Street

Poems by Tim Staley

To Carole,
Thanks for
Coming!

Tim Staley

7.25.16

for Suzanne

Contents

The Best Drops of Him

Off Hold

Lost On My Own Street

for Sean Branson 1977-2004

Last call sounded too much like a cowbell so we all kept dancing

A digital microwave technician stares straight at you when he sneezes

Hernando De Soto untied his robe each night before getting into bed

He never told me he had one lung nor did he predict the weather

The cardinal purpose of a big band is to swing, heaven is filled with
jazz singers, the dogs on the corner snap their claws

We thought it was him hunched over, across the street, underneath
the only cone of light

Even the locals in this puddle make love in the summer to near strangers

She felt like the inside of a new sweatshirt

I watched a tumbleweed roll around my yard for damn near an hour

The ceiling collapses in my bedroom and I choose to blame people

Out of spite, animals won't set you up to fail

General Jackson stands over the young man's body and weeps and exclaims,
I have lost the flower of my army

I keep looking at his pictures waiting to deluge

Practice means doing the same thing you just did

A Great Lake evaporates from the Atlantic every day

He got up to go to the bathroom, or the bedroom, when the vessel burst

Next week I'll turn my clock back, and the next week back again,
    and back again, until I wake up as I lie down

He used to be the fastest runner in school until his parents got divorced

He said poetry is crowd surfing and if we stop it'll bust its head

If you love your parents it's hard to tell them certain things

I don't think I'm strong enough to open the emergency exit so I ask
    the air steward if I can be moved

For a few seconds, the wind was a pack of dogs divided by a grid of mutual
    fences all coughing and hacking, a cacophony of someone's passing

Rules

The Complete Idiot's Guide to Getting Pregnant

Sniff a glue stick twenty minutes pre-coitus.
No cayenne, missionary position, or bike seats,
though our friends from The Netherlands
swear a hair of UB40 and cocaine works.
The sculptor's daughter says stop trying,
she centrifuged spooge for years,
wed an optimistic soothsayer,
but not until her dad died
did her mind kick start a heart.
Be done with thinking in the moment
is how crackheads and teens do it.
Jojo says okra is God's gift to placenta
and she got knocked up with two broken legs.
Don't forget your Co-Op cocktail:
Golden flower, Mucinex, shavings of chrome,
L-carnitine, vitamin E, THC, omega 3,
kiwi zest, emergency Xanax, and flaxseed.
JB says squeeze your butt cheeks
when you skeet, skeet, skeet—
says pants to the right side's a boy.
Grandma says keep your pants on,
rest on a bed of unrefined sugar,
get acupunctured by the spears of palm trees.
Oh, forget that woo-woo bullshit.
New Age is ancient, Caesar threw his
barren wife at a foot racer to shake off
her sterile curse, Saturn ate his kids.
            Whatever you do, do it religiously.
After ejaculation attach your wife
to the ceiling with gravity boots,
smudge her belly with moxa roll

atop a fine slice of ginger root
held at 140 degrees Fahrenheit
for six hours and twenty-six minutes.

Most important, you can't be stressed out.
The more years that pass, the more you relax.
The more you want it, the more you mustn't
imagine a little you in the world, swinging
into his terrible threes, screaming phrases
you so tirelessly taught him, hamming it up
in hazardous ways—Blot him out!

Sleep late in a quiet house.
Let your wife chase down-feathers
in the back room, so light
they elude her broom, suspend
in a rectangle of sun.

Direct Objects

Zulema is far too made-up
and props her fuzzy boots
on Carlos' desk. She says
her mom would take

care of one if she had a baby.
Zulema is far too sexy for our
discussion of direct objects.
She says her friend Rosario

is in the desert right now,
behind the soccer fields
on a dusty mattress
with José who already has a baby.

She has Carlos' attention and mine.
I don't tell her I met my wife
at the fertility clinic this morning
and in a cold room masturbated

into a clear, sterile container.
Zulema sucks the straw
of her Sonic cup until it rattles.
She sets the Styrofoam on the floor

and chews and twiddles the straw
until it's time to go. Out the window
comes José strutting from the desert
across the soccer fields; his pants

permanent press. His sweater maroon and tightly spun.

Cracker Ceremony

Repeat after me:

I do not want to remain a child forever.
Today is the day I become an adult.

I understand once I graduate I will no longer
receive Special Education services

for my Behavioral and/or Emotional Disorder.
I promise to act like an adult in every class.

The teacher will help me become an adult
as one day I may be his neighbor.

This cracker I hold in my hand
is a symbol for my life.

Break the cracker in half

Silently, repeat after me:

In breaking this cracker in half
I am breaking from my childhood.

I am an adult now so I can tell the crumbs
on the desk and floor will have to be vacuumed.

If Cracker Ceremony makes my eyes water,
the teacher won't count it as crying.

The primary ingredient, unleavened flour,
rose from the dust like everyone else.

Dead doves and living weeds are just as
pressing when they happen on my property.

I pledge allegiance to the mindset of cut grass
completely through with who wounded who.

Smoke

A tangle of hormone and saxophone
  when braces at trumpets scrape
  when the bell of them is thrown up
like a cheerleader no one's left to catch

When her water
breaks her plans for afternoon
and puddles at my desk
  I race to the restroom mirror
to see from my ears the rich
sinewy smoke of a crematorium

When I let them go
they swipe blindly at each other's
  sex parts, cries half bovine/half bird
infect the intercom, signal alarm

Strange scents in the lounge
too many to manage, Ms. Mitchell
again mentions cut roses,
I still like them, she says,
even though they're broken
and burning from the inside out.

The Clammy Handshake

Just because you restrain your dog doesn't make you a good parent

When the airbag exploded, the girl driving Carlos' truck didn't expect
    the second-degree burns on her hands and arms

In the pecan orchard along Don Juan de Oñate Trail, men in heavy yellow
    equipment use joysticks to manipulate giant saws and the trees recognize
    the men are not to be trifled with

The girl had not borrowed Carlos' truck to take her sick baby to the hospital
    like she said, she borrowed it to steal a bottle of rum

Carlos skips his afternoon classes to make out with his girlfriend, month
    after month, and I ask him, *is your boner worth more than your diploma*,
    teachers ask the stupidest questions

Oñate made two hundred and sixteen promises before he crossed the Rio Grande

During second period Carlos lent a girl his blue truck because she said her baby
    needed the hospital and her baby had a bad heart already

I never think about the bullet hole in my bedroom window

Laughing the girls were passing the rum they'd lifted, heading back
    to school for lunch

The teacher was talking to Mom about Carlos' bad behavior and I felt
    in the teacher's voice the quavering restraint of tears

The dog next door will not stop barking because he needs your help understanding
    the pros and cons of barking

The teacher's hands were shaking and bright red

From the impact, the girl in the passenger seat of Carlos' truck went through
the windshield, flying briefly before being airlifted to Thomason

In Rio de Janeiro, 1966, my father saw in a busy road—ten feet from the curb—
the obvious bulge of a human body, it was under a white sheet
surrounded by candles

In case you were wondering, there were no grab bags at the party

Carlos told me at the urinals he didn't really care about the accident,
about the lawsuit, about the girl in the hospital, he just doesn't
care anymore

Mothers on the Oñate Trail, over house gowns, wear gaudy NFL jackets
and wait at the ends of their long gravel driveways for the school bus
to deliver their children

RULES

1

Adam, coming in or out, slams the heavy door to my classroom—
it echoes down D Hall. I tell him there's no book on bipolar or
ADHD that says no patience is a symptom. My intention is to use
words on Adam, and if that doesn't work, I'll use words on Adam.
He's my white kid in second period with skulls on the tongues of
his tennis shoes. One day he secures a heavy duty zip tie around his
neck and his face turns blue. The zip tie is too tight, too thick for
me to cut. I put the scissors back in the cup; Carlos takes them and
tries harder. My pedagogy: ask less, expect less—I'm not saying it'll
work for you. Adam says, *fuck this school, nobody likes me, you don't
either, people say I can graduate, why should I?* Adam says, *I have no
patience,* he says, *my mom says I don't,* and he's up in my face. The
precious AP kids are doing their college testing next door, and the
AP teachers keep shitting themselves because I don't have Adam's
door slamming under control. I tell them, *that's the way it is.*

2

On the AP field trip to California
each senior got a shot of Crown Royal.
The eight of them like a giant squid
sprawled across the beds. The bottle
never left the teacher's hand, she moved
slowly to each one. She lifted the rim
to their lips. She wiped their mouths
with a paper towel. The kids were happy
and no one in the whole room was thinking
about helium, about how it's so hard
to replace.

3

A security guard was supposedly standing right there
when Zulema called 911 from my telephone.

I heard paramedics and the Assistant Principal
burst through my door right when Zulema was saying,
I saw a lion with down Syndrome on the internet.

I was there, right there, just standing around
thinking about the 331 cubic miles of water
that evaporate from the earth each day. About how
half those miles never get roped into clouds.

Home, Sweet

turn left on Rosa Parks
right on MLK
Taco Bell's on the left

All of my heroes are dying.

The birds are fighting crazy today.
The pileated woodpecker sprays bark
from his frenzied beak,
house finches squabble and flap
over seed, and the doves
joust the dog's bowl for a drink.

There is a pound of volcanic rock
in my stomach.

For Vivian Malone Jones,
just to register for class,
it took National Guard bayonets
to prod Alabama's governor aside
and now, she's dead and
what business do I have missing her?
She never sat in Sports Illustrated
afloat a tide of white shoulders.

This week five churches in Alabama
were razed to the ground and
it was raining the day of the boycott
and now
that voice is runoff,
somewhere in the darkness,
somewhere
deep in the cording.

The Fumble

A plumed and yellow bruise
so many cleats fell through.
The grass waits
under a two-pound ball.

The cheerleaders scream,
fly, and feel guilty
though the men spotting
say they shouldn't.

The ref's under a hood
replaying the instant,
but did you know most of his eyes
aren't even there for seeing?

The color commentator
paints words blue, pink,
then removes both
in steady swipes of solvent.

The play-by-play commentator
says one out of three
passes ends in fumble.
The ref is still under the hood

and until he forces down
the public address button
on his pelvis, his call rolls
and tumbles like a quarter in outer space.

Soon they'll see the ball
without a heartbeat for themselves
when the stands are empty,
save a few plastic shards,

and the parking lot's empty,
and the dumpsters, empty,
no boy or girl, just a wishbone
broken perfectly in half.

Redshirt

Gonzalo spins a rifle in front of his face
so fast it blurs like a propeller.

Rifles twirling above your head
in the high school parking lot
can be life-affirming but catching them
hurts. Gonzalo broke his finger last spring,
today the sight coming down
caught his cheek like a serrated knife
catches a homegrown tomato.

Blood soaks his shirt.
His red spoor in the parking lot,
the grass, the sidewalk, the threshold
down the long tiled hallway
to the boys' room where he presses
a wet paper shell to his wound.
He didn't cry with his finger
and he doesn't cry now.

In three minutes he'll be deployed
into my class to sit beside Ole
his cousin who's crying today
who can't write his name today
another concussion today
the fourth time his brain ricocheted
against the bone of his skull
in the name of the football team.

His rifle is American clip-loaded,
5-round magazine fed, bolt-action.

The only difference between
his standard-issue ROTC rifle
and the real one is the solid barrel,
from the factory they weigh the same.

Still I wonder if Gonzalo
will ever write poems
about what it's like to kill a man.

Inside Job

Inside the Co-Op Market of Las Cruces
we seal bags of raw basmati rice
to send to the President of the United States
so he can weigh them in his hands
and drop them with bombers instead of bombs.

My brother will be the first wave
to break upon Baghdad.
He'll rub a canker sore against his incisor
just to feel alive.
He's never loaned me anything
not even for a minute.

I punch numbers into the cash register
when a customer says his first calculator
cost him 600 dollars, a Texas Instrument,
it blinked when it was thinking and I'm digging
for a scrap of paper so pleased
another grain of minutiae
has dropped from the ether
when the mailman trudges in returning
all the bags of raw basmati rice.

My next customer's shirt says, *Give War a Chance*
which brings me to the 1960s
when hippies burned down my father's ROTC building.
Yes, this peace sign matches my satchel,
but what else?

I hardly know my brother
staring down at empty shells

clanking and shuffling on the tank floor.
Through the rectangle window
a column of dust streams in
like the dirtiest spotlight
with no radio, no mirror ball,
no Crosby Stills Nash or Young,
no sound of the ocean at work
deep inside those shells.

Ode to Catastrophe

Jack says on Halloween the living and dead mingle.
We're lucky the plastic masks hide our friends' faces.
So much gore on the highway today, cops draw a curtain.
Police identify victims as mother and son, next time
maybe you'll be the one drawn to the wreckage,
diving for your family in the flames, unable
to separate your fingers from their grim details.
A congregation of smoke above the interstate,
the roads themselves are wilting, hirsute with flesh.
With white chalk I trace the asphalt sinew, silhouettes
settle like salt on my tongue, like the errant blood
in Ryan's brain—here, here's a tissue, a collective
catastrophe we don't depend on like death,
too liquid to pin down, it's mist in every footprint.
It's the Grim Reaper's costume jewelry, it's gravel
in the pit of our stomach. It's slippery
when someone's dying means you're *not* dead,
and it's nothing personal. We fly lightly
like a gnat until we don't, and refuse
to rejoice with trembling. One day
you're Beatlick Joe, high stepping
on the panhandle, and the next
Day of the Dead I'm setting a Tecate
on your altar. I feel the marrowless bones like
peanut butter in my throat, Tootsie Rolls in my
windpipe. My doorbell rings and rings, and it's a miracle
nobody's there. I study the field mice who leave
their tiny bolts and screws on my kitchen floor, who pass
their desperate microphone from one mouth to another.

Cusp of Snow and Thaw

Just Listen

Nowadays it's our instinct
to fill our brains with foreground sounds
whether it be a woman's voice
cutting into you or chainsaws,
weed whackers, lawnmowers.

It's hard even once you're in the wilderness
to quit your brain from replaying
that scene from the hall
where a sibling stood shattered
or even a folk song
don't you know me?
I'm your native son.

Listening to nature is like
listening to a poem. You have to put your
precious thoughts on standby
so you might understand someone else's.

We turn our backs on nature
even when we're up against it.
I can't quit my brain long enough
to let the shadow of the canyon
give way to warmth, to the
creek's purr, to the squawk
of the Steller's jay, to the soundtrack
of the fire's cracks
resolving in one last lace
of blue flame
dancing, zigzagging,
ducking into coals.

Do You Feel Alright

When Bob Marley Jr. asks the crowd,
do you feel alright? I take it personally.
I ask my friend how she feels alright
and she suggests a six pack before bed
but there are bubbles in beer and I know
feeling bloated isn't feeling alright.
I shoot numerous arrows toward God
bent over like a question mark and after
no word from the celestial bondsman,
I go local, drink a few flat beers and write
the president in a calm cursive.
He gets back to me quickly
with an autographed 8X10 and I feel
alright for a while but I'm
not sure because he never stops
smiling and that's suspicious.
I ask my wife, *do I feel alright?*
and she's tying the laces of her
Jazzercise shoes really tight as she
doesn't want them falling off
when she's dancing. I call my mom
and before I even finish asking
she says, *yes, yes, you feel alright*
and you feel handsome too,
and I do feel handsome for a while
so I restring my racquetball racket
and speed walk the food court
but I don't feel alright, so I
ask my brother and he says,
I got to get out of here, so I go
to the nearest forest and shut the door.

I follow a stream all the way up
a mountain into the cold mist
and feel my toes and fingers
go numb and feel myself fall in
the windblown scattering of peaks.

The Hanging Gardens

And in a way don't we all end up
in the Aleutians playing an acoustic
Shelter from the Storm at The Hotel
open mic and isn't there always a girl
giving or taking the eye and the fishermen
like any tourists snapping the town to pieces
leaving busted stitches on the floor
and you don't hear what you're singing
but in the refrain you're far from lonely
and the melody tumbles from your guitar
like The Hanging Gardens and hey
maybe you're not Dylan but at this vector
it doesn't really matter and who knows
the Hawaiian waitress may
take you home so many times
it's no big deal anymore and you
start to miss when you didn't have her
didn't have exactly what you'd asked for
but there was always gas in the tank
and freedom to go and you'd never
consider being Nebuchadnezzar
building a green mountain in the desert
just to cheer up a girl.

To Re-Spark Love

These desert peaks are gushing
two miles up from the parking lot.
This charging water, that could stop
any second, is three feet deep in places
and notes the sun with sparkles.
How much of this will I remember
come the anvil of summer
to deaden our passions,
come the inevitable searing
of these same river stones?

On a wave of red wine
a bee rides into my mouth.
Her sparkle of wings
for a second on my tongue.
Her stinger's no match
for my stomach.

I hover on the sounds of the stream.
The sun touches the top
and bottom of every sparkle.
Could sparkles be the placeholders
and not the place?

Neatly Under the Current

A silver donkey on her side
gives birth on the banks
to something still. I'm happy
for her the push is over.
Her relaxed breath
echoes quietly

down the canyon.
With a branch
I shove the heap
neatly under the current.
Fifty feet later, a ribcage
for a moment in the sun.

Leaving the Aldo Leopold Wilderness

After nine nimble days
in statuesque snow
I turn us home.
My dog splashes
on vivid red paws
across the Mimbres
and up the canyon.
I'm calmed by the
one-sided challenge of
the climb, with a sixty
pound pack I'm
floored by momentum.
From the mountain
I emerge again reset,
my strata of concerns
rolled back to tranquil.
If my truck had started
and lumbered us down
the forest road
High Lonesome Radio
could have come in
fuzzy at first, Christmas
a day away, bombs
going off in mosques,
and Condoleezza could say
something, but it doesn't start
and we're put to sleep
as snow darkens
the windshield.

Wasted Nights

Again I stand in the backyard waiting
for dog eyes to shine like green dimes.
I envy the clear New Mexico sky,
the moon a new size shows stars
how bright to be. I think, here I am
wasting away another night, if only
I was really under it: the cliff face,
the icy stream, the small fire
inside a circle of stones.

One-Track Mind Conflicted

Josh and I hiked yesterday
to where the Rio Grande swallows the Red,
600 cubic feet of fast water
hardly coerced by 30 more.

Two kayakers pull out a half klik
upriver from our camp and fling
their boats on their backs and zip
the mile straight up to the rim of the canyon.
There's a cooler of cold beer in their car
and they're not going home, they're going to the Chama,
the Yampa, the Colorado, the Buffalo,
the Chattooga, the Coosa, the Tallapoosa...

Josh and I are quiet for days
like the black basalt boulders
that slowly sink in the Rio's banks
like dying worms with one-track minds
that know they should disintegrate
but keep on digging anyway.

I know I should return to where I started
but need to keep feeling this brush
of pine needles against my cheek, this wisp
of lightning, these battered clouds
facing off the New Mexico sun.

The Snow Covered You Up

for Sean Branson 1977-2004

The snow covered you up
and I thought after hiking the spine
of the Continental Divide
and down the Atlantic side
and up the Mimbres to you
we could dance again
like we used to,
like puppets, our bones
loose in our skin.

On the Cusp of Snow and Thaw

I tell myself I'm home out here
alone in the cold
a half mile from the road
beside Sapillo Creek
where silence broods
on the nailhead of the moon
without budging.

Each night the freeze
stretches out the earth's pores
and leaves them worn out
and satisfied in the morning.

Tonight Old Forester sloshes
in my blue aluminum cup
while Willie Nelson sings
from a tiny speaker:
One night of love
can't make up
for six nights
*alon*e. I romanticize
man versus wild
while hundreds of miles away
on our crappy futon
there's a wilderness
in my wife's eyes
I can't face.

I'm drunk enough now
to appreciate anywhere
there's water in the air,
I hear it ticking to ice.

A hound dog
with a transmitter collar
trots through my camp
on a mission.
He goes deeper
into the wilderness
than I care to.
Maybe
I'm not ready
for so much quiet.

The Sickness Suite

The Birth Story

It's no big deal

today feels

its gags on the treetops.

Opens by the centimeter

from shallow nap

at the end of a tunnel.

She isn't super impressed

like the first baby

who just sits there.

No one can wait

for strain in her anus.

Erupts around her

a yellow cauliflower

of cactus paddles

screaming

like next week.

The starwild dark

between her legs.

Deep in the canal

a cloud of bats.

I say visualize.

I say sterling skullcap.

I say quivering.

Is yesterday

New Mexico

whose tomorrow

a mucus canoe?

I'm not sleep-deprived

Nova Scotia or Telluride.

Crabby with the midwife.

A bag of waters

a scrape at the crate

a yellow flood

12:45.

What *is* that?

Someone else's hair.

Maybe I'm Merlin

to thrashes.

Whoever invented

Natural Childbirth

is a fucking idiot.

The sun won't

in firelight

without words

in misty forest

born in orbit

above our house

the Curve of Carus.

I break

careen and screech.

Splashes

in the backyard.

A shatter

of moonlight

I step into.

I step into

a shooting star.

Someone Whose Mind Watches Itself

Wobbly eyed in a car
chasing Sylvia's ambulance
to El Paso.

My friend Jesse, a then Buddhist,
told me to rise above my thoughts
high enough
to look down.

> So I'm above myself
> in the cold
> still chasing
> Sylvia's ambulance
> to El Paso.

I feel something like a tarantula walking around in my stomach.

I was never sitting in a teacup
waiting for a ride, I just landed
in the long arm of a spin.

After
after twenty
twenty hours
a doctor with his bottom teeth in braces says, *for some reason she's
shutting down.*

> I saw a man
> go from swept under a dam,
> to bobbing face down,
> to hands outstretched,
> to slowly spinning.

I saw myself seeing him,
how selfish, I thought,
he's ruining the whole river.

I wanted to help,
I saw myself helping,
just never did.

On the top floor of the hospital there's an ice cream machine that leaks
Dreamsicle. I spin across the tile like a cat's eye marble and my eyes
stay open like marbles.

Dear Buddha,
I've been praying
to myself
like you taught me.

I tell my wife,
it'll never stop,
she says, *please,*
stop talking.

My guts erupt, out pours the black thread of my bellybutton.
It comes and comes, collects at my feet, sticks to my knees, gets harder
and harder to hide from the nurses, doctors, and priest.

Sylvia nurses peacefully in Suzanne's lap while I sit in the corner
and spool my darkness.

To the basement
for Sylvia's nuclear scan,
the tech guy, nice enough, asks,
is she your only child?

A clock radio in the corner isn't quite loud enough.

Pruning the Agaves

A comet of freeze slams our backyard white—

    shuts ants in their tunnels, locks bile
    in the ducts, blocks with ice her portal vein

    makes succulents messy puppets
    stretched yellow against the snow.

    Before the freeze their heads were fierce spires
    with time to hoist their panicles of yellow flowers.

    Now she's hoarse with shrieking, I hear her
    between the blows of my shovel, into the rot

    I slosh my blade, she fades, is that
    our phone ringing? is it Houston? do they

    have a liver? is the jet on the way?
    I keep hauling agaves to the dumpster,

    they smell of tequila and vomit, yellow ooze
    stains my gloves. Suzanne stalls on the threshold,

    says, *spring is coming*, but it's not to us
    the promise of spring is made.

The Waiting Game

1

Vikings never ask are we there yet,
they just scan the horizon, armored hips against the railing

It's nothing where you see the end
like the line for a roller coaster

It's nothing like Russian roulette,
or even regular roulette

And Vikings suck at sneaking up,
branches rattle their helmets,
not to mention
their laughter

2

It's true, one day the Operating Room nurses will take her
down a far-off hall
where she'll get smaller
and smaller in their arms
until they turn a corner
and assemble around her
to open her belly
like the bow of a Viking ship
opens the sea

3

And you go to sleep with waiting
and rise with it curdled on your tongue

Or bracing for the Mississippi to crest
thirty-two miles from shore

Or waiting for a B positive liver
to be delivered
to Texas Children's Hospital,
Houston, room twelve
twenty-two

4

Several nurses and doctors will tell you, *it's a waiting game,*
and that cheers you up
like a salt lens three miles wide
cheers up the sea

Vikings, like anyone, can't help that rush of pressure
up from their hearts to their helmets,
but don't worry,
you can write poems
instead of crying

5

And by now you're wishing the phone would ring with an offer,
with a liver to swirl from one body of water to another

When Vikings don't have phones,
they use screaming
and fire

6

It's not waiting for a hangover to recede
or swimming with your mouth open
or a ride to Rothko Chapel
where maybe under the onus of art
you'll find God

It's not Leif Erikson but *The Wreck of the Hesperus,*
your daughter bound to the mast in a hurricane

And it's official those are eagles
circling her steel crib,
they're here to claw out her liver,
and each day it grows back
they're back again

7

It's not Eastern medicine or Western or talking to the trees
or crossing the street when you're not supposed to,
it's a butterfly in a blizzard
and a satellite looking down

If only you could stop noticing
it's a hospital room
under an ocean of bile and the nurses
laughing at your spine like a dorsal fin,
swishing, breaking the surface

If only your heart was broken,
how easy life would be

"Untitled"

The hospital walls are hung with children's paintings,
all of them "Untitled" but they're clearly an ocotillo,
a pit bull, and some stupid crepe paper parachute.
I blame the art teachers, isn't it their job to know what's what?

In Pär Lagerkvist's book entitled *The Sibyl*,
a woman wakes up in a cave after giving birth,
she sees something bloody and slimy between her legs,
she sees goats eagerly licking it clean with their long, pink tongues.

It's been 14 days in the airplane chairs of the waiting room,
43 in the hospital, and 95 since diagnosis. Two weeks ago they sliced
under the arc of her ribcage and lifted out her liver, they wheeled it
across the street for Baylor to magnify 15,000 times, to find "Untitled."

Beside the aquarium, fully reclined in the airplane chair,
I have a dream Pär and I are mixing concrete in a rusted wheelbarrow,
I'm holding the hose and we don't talk about the goats as he stirs
the concrete with a shovel, his gray hair tosses in the breeze.

Noxious gas pumps from the hoses attached to the wall,
the doctors gyrate and speak in tongues. I say, *I always knew
this type of pain was out there, now it's just ours to taste,*
and it's phrases like this that drive my wife crazy.

The woman in the cave tried to tear the navel cord, and finding
she couldn't, bit it in two and took the child in her arms to keep it
from the goats. When my lap child comes to, she'll find hot water bags
for lungs, a plastic vent down her throat, her arms strapped to the rails.

I wish I was a crossing guard, a bright swirl of hands, arms, whistles—
clean gestures for go and stay. I'm with Pär on the banks
of the Castalian Spring. I can name every grain of sand, I can see a place
where they whirl gently around, moved by an invisible finger.

One In, One Out

In the waiting room
parents recline together,
some scream at the TV in ecstasy
as their Dallas Mavericks
alley-oop, fast break,
and foul the Miami Heat
for the NBA title.
In the other corner
a couple is told
by a surgeon in scrubs
their baby has a tumor
in her brain.
I'm not a sports fan
so I notice the husband
shake, cry, and pout.
His wife says,
it's going to be hard…
I put in ear plugs, draw
the hood of my sweatshirt
clean over my eyes.

The Transplant

I wasn't looking for a liver or thinking about livers, I was look-
ing for a Texas crescent, a cloudless sulphur, a tropical checkered
skipper, or even a measly old monarch, but that day the butterflies
weren't presenting in the Butterfly Garden. I looked in every spider
web. I found a fountain that was too clean. I watched a woman
with a hospital nametag float from one rosebud to another snipping
as she went. I followed a line of ants to a dead pigeon. They were
dancing on her eyes, singing *Kumbaya* in a circle, they'd waited
and waited. They lifted their tiny cups of blood to the mirrored
buildings sparkling all around, and I thought about the time I
was driving a country highway from Tuscaloosa to Montgomery,
when I was convinced I had cause enough to turn my wheel to the
headlights zipping toward me. How easy it would be to cross those
yellow lines, to flit over the border.

Ronald McDonald House

It's Monday and the Junior League Harvester Ants
spread out their fruit before me to dry: melons,
peaches, spaghetti, iceberg lettuce,
and little cups of Hidden Valley Ranch.
They don't know where to find a liver.

It's Tuesday and the Honey Ants of Southwest Airlines
lug in to plug in their piña colada machine and I nurse
its frigid spin and the DJ plays Steven Stills
on ridiculous speakers and TJ rests his head
on the table, then there's a photograph

of his pregnant sister in a bikini, her bulbous midriff
in a field of sleepy daisies, it's lovely like Pine-Sol.
I close up at night like a daisy. The Army Ants
of Anesthesiology cross their eyelashes into mine,
I sleep in coliseums as their columns march by.

For a week the shuttle floats empty to the hospital.
For a week we dream of home, of the boric acid
under the armoire, of baby copperheads
in the rat traps, babies without a handle
on how much poison to let fly.

A Jaundiced View

At Kinley's House Coffee & Tea,
a girl in flirty flats slides in next to me,
her liver functioning perfectly, her blood
clotting like batter in a waffle iron. A family
strolls in, mom and three kids, their gallbladders
all draining, filling and tipping
bile as they should except dad forgot his wallet.
Has to walk all the way back to his Hummer,
the capillaries in his liver robust, nothing
like my daughter's liver, a jellyfish skewered
on a cactus spine. She's with my wife nearby
wrestling infection in the nosocomial claw
of the hospital, where my baby's veins
are gateways to super germs who've united,
who've built up resistance to antibacterial
disinfectants and I wish I had that gall,
that crass resilience.

The Best Drops of Him

In the Water House

Water boards keep wheatgrass nails growing

       I keep the walls free of eddies
            of water spiders too

A vapor trail rises from the chimney

Down the stairs I glide
           a canoe for slippers
               a paddle for a cane

Trigger fish in the hallway
koi in the windowsill

As one summer
       rotates into another
       I roll on parquet waves
       in otiose slumber

       The telephone's sunk

               Sunsets blanch

          Rings rise in colorful bubbles

              and die in quiet splashes

On Her First Birthday

She falls down
she falls down
we follow after
you're ok
you're ok.

I remember
handing her over
to the nurses
seeing her clueless
through a window
down a long hall
smaller and smaller
in their arms.

Last weekend
a boy wandered off
from his family
got lost in the dunes
of White Sands.
Two days later
they found him
he said he'd been
following a bubble
one that kept floating
just out of reach.

The Ramifications of Escape

If I could go anywhere with anyone I'd go
to sleep. I'd worm my way to the footboard
and dream of someone new, someone to kiss
feverishly until she's across the table from me
in a cheap sweater on the outskirts of Budapest,
lowering her eyes, keeping them down,
toying with me, it's exquisite and sexual
in a refreshing way, and everything's
great until one of the gypsies in the corner
puts his fiddle down and says, *if you see
the Danube as blue you're in love,*
but there's no window, no doors,
no river, feverishly I search all night.
I'm never awakened by the dawn
or the alarm, the trashman or the grappler,
my wife or the battery-operated
aural weaponry of our three-year-old.

Audrey Hepburn in a Plastic Frame

Come quick, they cry, *the moon's exploding!*
Only it doesn't explode, it just sheds a layer.

Moonskin drifts down through the clouds
empty as dragonfly shells,
gray as dandelion seed.

I hear this dream
from my daughter's hairdresser
who doesn't like her thighs or Jessica Alba

or this little town which isn't small at all.
I see Broadway hand-tinted and framed
on her wall: taxicabs, *The Color Purple*
and more marquees in the distance,
an accordion of monochrome buildings
beneath a sheen of shellac.

My daughter's hair
falls about the hairdresser's feet.
My daughter sits still
like she never does for me.

I studied ballet for ten years,
the hairdresser says, *up until*
my sophomore year of high school.

For once I'm not thinking about sex or the lack
of circulation in this room. I'm just
listening to dreams.

Vagina Ear

On a sunny morning my wife informs me
my ear smells like a vagina.
Delighted, I stroke my index finger
down from the helix, past the canal to lobe,
and finally to nose. At long last
God has answered my prayer.

At three o'clock in the high school parking lot
I kneel on a red velvet pillow.
My ear tilted, unmuffed,
and ready to receive the long train
of boys and one curious girl.
No touching, I warn them
as I stuff their dollars in my pouch.

That weekend no one mentions it
on the guys' canoe trip down the river
but they all wind up in my tent.
Their cold pink noses fanned out
like spokes from my ear.

Then every day a different discharge:
stringy, gooey, gritty,
stretchy, slimy, itchy,
vinegary, an elevator of mucus,
a crescendo of blood. I never heard
there was so much to love.

The 10 Commandments
of the Second-Wave Men's Movement

Thou shalt funnel all unfulfilled sexual desire into a hobby of your choosing.

Thou shalt hide alone in the snowy woods between Christmas and New Year's.

Thou shalt say you're sorry at exactly the same time.

Remember to relax the sphincter of your ego at least once a week.

Honor electricity, even though it makes the stupid mistake of circling back.

Thou shalt never masturbate in someone else's shoes.

Thou shalt never feel obliged to provide your orgasms an audience.

Thou shalt never forget men have mammary glands too.

Thou shalt smile politely when Savannah says, *Men's Movement my ass.*

Thou shalt please pick up the big stuff, any doofus shalt handle the little stuff.

The Best Drops of Him

Imagine a new father on a park bench,
in his lap his baby is latching on,
it's true, this baby is chestfeeding.

Women love to keep men's dugs in the dark,
they don't want us to know
we have milk ducts, mammary tissue,
oxytocin, prolactin, all the hormones
needed to brew milk in our own body,
even American men do.

The new father feels the weight
of his left pec start to lessen,
he shifts the babe from one nipple
to the other, natural, magical.

I'm not saying it's easy or popular,
and I can't speak to the nutritional value,
but he stimulated his nipples
for several hours each day, usually
after work, but sometimes
in the teacher's lounge. His poor
nipples, two swollen gherkins
rolled between fingers for months
and months before even a drop,
the slightest drop, but Oh!
what a drop it was,
it tasted like onion.

The new father sits in a folding chair
next to the new mother at the milk bank.

Both are hooked up to the pump.
There's no talking, it doesn't matter.
Some balance at last between them.
It's 3 AM and outside the children's hospital
Fannin Street is quiet.

Ed

Ed died and we gather bowls of guacamole at his home.
I see his tools, his workshop, his engine parts,
his pint glasses stuffed with pens and markers
and his daughter jerked from her own monotony
to decide on all these things.

Ed had just taken a shower, was in a towel on his bed,
glasses in his hand, not a drop of liquor in his system,
a bead of blood left a wobbly line beneath his nose.
He'd been cleaning up for a party he'd never get to

as if the liquor had been saving him...
only a user would say that.
I use as many chips as I can, we all do,
still the guacamole grays and blackens
faster than we can finish.

Playing Twenty Questions with God

Are you a cop

Do my parents know
I'm a mosquito

Is my wife still having fun

Are you still having fun
so many places at once

Was I intentionally left blank

Will I die in a drive-by shooting
sitting on my sofa, bullets right
through my back

Are you like Jeopardy
where the answers
are the questions

Are you a car that steers itself

Are you a palindrome

Are you down with capitalism

Did you pick this restaurant

Are those your cheese fries

Can I have some

Are you crawling around the sky,
right now,
like an airplane

Are you that far away

After the Big Bang
did you barf

Is it true
there's a naked lady,
spinning around
inside every atom

Is mittelschmerz real

Am I getting warmer

Are you what a puddle leaves
when it's done

Rose Colored Dreams

Rose Colored Dreams booked a room at the Ramada Palms.
He checked in as soon as he could and hardly felt his feet
touch the ground. He noticed bright flowers in the flowerpots,
too bright to be real, but he loved them as his brothers.

Rose Colored Dreams went to Walmart to buy some Armor All.
He went to the one that was until recently the newest, the one
on Valley Drive. He took a job there in order to write a novel,
investigative reporter style, he sucked pennies to calm his nerves,
he spent all his time watching them watch him.

Rose Colored Dreams went on a date with Compromised Dreams,
and you wouldn't believe it, Deferred Dream was their waiter.
He had a lisp. He didn't write anything down, he was that good.
Rose Colored Dreams spent the night talking about his penis
and all the other barnacles dragging his ego down.

Rose Colored Dreams heard bad news came in threes, then learned
the hard way. He never saw Compromised Dreams again, her work
kept her busy, but he didn't buy it. She had a little mouth
and he told everybody about it, he'd hold his hand in a tight fist
and say her mouth was that little.

Rose Colored Dreams almost died in a car wreck 14 miles long,
he did misplace his eyes that day. His car was in ruin
for weeks. He couldn't laugh at his sorrows
because he didn't know he was more than sorrow,
he was special, very special.

The Proposition

I sat next to him. I hugged him
and began to cry, saying how much
I missed him. He said she gave him
a straightforward proposition. *Is she
God?* I asked. He said, *of course.*
He felt no remorse about deciding
to fly off that back road into trees.
He said he lives in a small town
which gave me the impression
he had time to listen.

Off Hold

To a Spider

for Sean Branson 1977-2004

See, it'll happen like this:
        when I dim the lights
        she'll unhook her safety line
        so I can put her back
        where she's never been.
        My drinking glass
        down around her crown
        as magic carpet slips
        between floor, rim,
        under eight limbs
        until cage and foundation
        are one I levitate,
        sure not to be jiggling
        her red hourglass
        through the living room, and when
        the glass ambulance lifts,
        from the paper stretcher she'll step
        to the perimeter of my property
        and probably, that snake
        won't eat her, and that wind,
        why should it freeze?
And in this way Sean, I wish I'd saved you
and your dog from circling your body for days
until finally she's stuck, whiskers
hard pressed against the window.

Observing Insects with my Toddler

In the backyard we brush a leaf
and touch some ticks and they, in turn,
touch us, resolute in their mindfulness.
I fetch the fire and Sylvia screams
as the match head licks the tick
and sizzles the peach fuzz on her leg.

A column of black ants aren't caught up
in their mind's chatter, in fact,
they're only attached to what they carry,
I admire that. She keeps smashing them.

Do ants bite? she asks.

No, only the red ones.

A huge roach writhes on its back,
another victim of chemical warfare.
A lightweight vestment of guilt,
light as a goose feather,
hangs on my shoulders
as I notice his dead brothers
strewn about the perimeter.

Are roaches mean? she asks.

No, just dirty.

50 Miles Outside Montgomery

Bald eagles have *hands* as wingtips
and spread open their fingers
like a businessman in a black suit
with black gloves who is starving.

His call is *weak, flat, stuttering,*
like he's being told to wait.
Don't get mad at me
I'm just quoting the bird book.

I'm not anti-eagle exactly,
there was one on the moon after all
with magnets for claws.

Clouds undress the sun
so I look at the red dirt
beside this newly painted road.
What shade of red
is watered-down Confederate blood?

50 miles outside Montgomery
on these shores of Lake Martin
you're either an organ pipe dirt dauber
who eats little spiders with triangles
on their backs, or you're the little spider
with a triangle on his back.

Hank Williams Sr. fished these same
lonesome sunsets
in a green aluminum boat.
Soon as stars spread

messy on the waves
he was crying for shore.

My dad says pine trees are grass
and I think he's lying.
The radio says lichen is fungus
and algae combined like a mule
locked for life to rocks and trunks.

A black speck above the green crown
grows as it approaches our floats.
A bald eagle, white head, black breast,
white tail, huge black wings,
the sky cradled in his fingers.
He passes too quickly to capture.

Match Point

A blue cup, a slobbered on
racquetball, a white beach towel
with red dots, a can of Bud Light
Koozied on its side, and the lake
lapping the battle ground.

One stings Sylvia in the eye
and swelling swallows it.
I stand there blinking, thinking
maybe she's beautiful this way
a unicorn of vision.

The cable guy says douse their nest in oil,
says pour till their last bubbles rise. My brother
says shove a Roman candle in their den, that'll
teach 'em. My dad tapes his socks to his trousers,
his sleeves to his gloves, a trash bag with eyes.

Me, I'll wait till they're drowsy,
till their yellow jackets are hung up by the door.
I'll recite for them a tone poem.
My lips press to their entrance
the best syllables.

Last Day in Alabama

Grass snake in the shower.
Turtle behind the fire house.
Imagine if the last thing you ever felt
was the grip of a spider web.
With sausage on the line
Sylvia reels a catfish
up from the dark.
We can't get the hook out.
He grins, takes matters into his own
razor fins, toddler blood
pools on the dock, Papa passes out,
and that snake—that pulsing
rivulet that slid over
my foot in the shower—
we locked him in a tackle box
for Sylvia to see in the morning
but somehow in the night
he jimmied the latch
and broke free.

Biosphere

Our house is a biosphere
sealed off from the outside world.
We're completely self-sufficient
once her anti-rejection meds
arrive in their own disposable cooler.

All the skylights keep singing
and we hold her leaves to the light.
We try our best to wipe away the pesticide
and the pollen of our misgivings.

Deep in the night she cries herself
back to sleep the way a morning glory
closes up shop in the heat of the day.

And each minute she escapes from us.
She asserts herself like oxygen
from a leaf and we stand there
thinking our skin is so thick,
thick like the skin of a bubble.

Blood Brother and Sister

I suggest my Bowie knife,
fresh slices to our palms,
an intersection of purple rivers.
You suggest my sewing kit.
The darning needle, I sanitize
with fire, you, with cotton balls
and alcohol. I say, *c'mon now, dig deep,*
we're only shedding symbolic blood here,
everybody knows that doesn't hurt.
Before each jab you inhale into a balloon
you can't bear to pop. I stab my ring finger
just below the knuckle, stand wide,
use my torso, ratchet so deep
a buoy of blood rises from my pinhole.
Our springs unwind under a purple bandana.
I wail ceremoniously and chant
about forever and you ask me how long.
The phone rings, a market researcher
questions my connection to Velcro.
I ask her, *are you anyone's blood sister?*
No, she says, *I'd never intentionally hurt myself.*

The Garment of Marriage

Avoid the rhythm of hand stitching,
choose the machine instead
for your garment of marriage,
favor two threads to needle,
two threads tensing up
to the same goal.

Sometimes the garment of marriage
is dry cleaned on a hanger
under a thin sheet of plastic in a closet.
If it dwells on the wrinkles of the past
leave it hanging, or teach it
to forgive itself its wrinkles.

Some days it's a dirty sock
lost under the dryer for years, decades even
until the dryer breaks and you're forced
to pull it out and there it is, you've found it,
you forgot how much you loved it.

Sometimes the bandana of marriage can
sail out the car window and float to the
shoulder like the female fluff of
cottonwoods on the gust of your
momentum up the mountain road where
a stream bed narrows into a peak
and the body of stars pulses with blood.

Duet

I play a song with Suzanne that has no chords
and walks on calendar days with felt-tip toes

I play a song with Suzanne alone in the woods

I play a song with Suzanne polished, the way
she likes to hear it, screaming from the shower
for love or some other implement of exfoliation

I play a song with Suzanne about ink, two white sheets
full of ink

I play a song with Suzanne that is a place,
an architecture of pastimes, car rides and
lazy nights, gas ups and faucets, all
the disobedient faucets

I play a song with Suzanne her shadow
let loose in the night

I play a song with Suzanne that tugs a house-size
helium balloon by its string and walks and sleeps with it
and tries never to let go

I play a song with Suzanne she doesn't always like

I play a song with Suzanne a soft current, will it
ground or keep charging the tubes of my gut

I play a song with Suzanne wrapped in a tortilla,
sprinkled with a bust of sunlight, and seasoned
by the Shawnee moon

I play a song with Suzanne I never listen to
at a polite distance

I play a song with Suzanne that is sometimes silent

I play a song with Suzanne that listens for a baby,
for another shot at love

I play a song with Suzanne with banjos,
Wurlitzers, trombones, and a big black
southern choir and all the people are
dancing and throwing their hands and
stomping and feeling better than they
did before

I play a song with Suzanne once I find
the spare key

Off Hold

These are the only times
humans aren't waiting:

orgasm, death,
sleeping, sneezing,
shitting, sprinting,
barfing, choking,
seizing, and maybe
if they're lucky
making art.

ACKNOWLEDGMENTS

I am grateful to the editors of the following publications, where these poems or earlier versions of them first appeared or are forthcoming:

"A Jaundiced View"	*Burnt District*
"Do You Feel Alright"	*Red Fez*
"Ed"	*Verse-Virtual*
"Home, Sweet"	*Las Cruces Poets & Writers*
"In the Water House"	*Cacti Fur*
"Just Listen"	*Las Cruces Poets & Writers*
"Kind to a Spider"	*Lunarosity*
"Last Day in Alabama"	*Ppig Penn*
"Lost On My Own Street"	*The Ink Spot*
"Leaving the Aldo Leopold…"	*Canary*
"Neatly Under the Current"	*Lively Words*
"Ode to Catastrophe"	*Beatlick News*
"One In, One Out"	*Bluegrass Accolades*
"One-Track Mind Conflicted"	*San Pedro River Review*
"On the Cusp of Snow…"	*Indiana Voice Journal*
"Playing Twenty Questions…"	*Owl Eye Review*
"Rose Colored Dreams"	*Cacti Fur*
"Rules"	*Damfino*
"Smoke"	*Cacti Fur*
"The Best Drops of Him"	*Crab Fat*
"The Clammy Handshake"	*Chaffey Review*
"The Complete Idiot's Guide…"	*RHINO: The Poetry Forum*
"The Ramifications of Escape"	*Spilt Ink*
"Wasted Nights"	*the Rag*

Special thanks to my mother, Joanne Staley.

Intimate thanks to my wife, Suzanne Staley.

Thanks to Lee Bartlett, Sheila Black, Sara Cooper, Wayne Crawford, Joaquin Fore, Peter Goodman, Pamela Hirst, Tony Hoagland, Dorine Jennette, New Mexico Arts, Night Ballet Press, Pski's Porch, Josh Robbins, Frank Sholedice, Joe Somoza, Joe Speer, Gerry Stork, Dick Thomas, Larry D. Thomas, Jim Thompson, Anna Underwood, Frank Varela, Connie Voisine, K. West and Ellen Young.